CITIES OF THE WORLD

LONDON

BY R. CONRAD STEIN

CHILDREN'S PRESS®
A Division of Grolier Publishing
New York London Hong Kong Sydney
Danbury, Connecticut

CONSULTANT

Harold Perkin
Professor of History and Higher Education
Northwestern University

Project Editor: Downing Publishing Services
Design Director: Karen Kohn & Associates
Photo Researcher: Jan Izzo

LIBRARY OF CONGRESS CATALOGING-IN-PUBLICATION DATA

Stein, R. Conrad.
 London / by R. Conrad Stein.
  p. cm. — (Cities of the world)
 Includes index.
 Summary: Describes the history, cultural composition, daily life, and points of interest of London.
 ISBN 0-516-00351-8
 1. London (England) — Juvenile literature. [1. London (England)]
I. Title. II. Series: Cities of the world (New York, N.Y.)
DA678.S85   1996
942.1—dc20   95-36156
                                                          CIP
                                                          AC

TABLE OF CONTENTS

Trafalgar Square is a large public plaza in the center of London. It is decorated with fountains and statues. For more than one hundred years, the square has been used for public gatherings. Many groups of people have met there to protest against some social evil. Shortly after World War II, protesters gathered to demand that Great Britain free her colonies in Asia and Africa.

Those colonies were once part of a British empire that stretched around the world. It was truly said that "The sun never sets on the British Empire." That huge empire broke apart after World War II, but the statues of Trafalgar Square are reminders of its former glory.

Bronze lions, the symbol of British power, guard the plaza. Towering over the grounds is a 170-foot column with a figure of Lord Horatio Nelson on the top. In 1805, Nelson commanded a British fleet that defeated the French and Spanish fleets. The battle took place near Cape Trafalgar on the coast of Spain. The victory made Britain the master of the seas. It made it possible for the nation to further expand its empire.

London became not only the capital of Great Britain, but also the leader of almost one-third of the globe. For more than 100 years, London was the world's largest city and one of its richest. Today, London's museums hold treasures from all the lands once touched by the British flag. The people of that long-ago empire are here, too. In modern London, one can eat an Indian dinner, watch a movie made in Pakistan, and listen to a Jamaican steel band all in the same evening. The mixture of different cultures and the rich history of the city makes the British capital one of the most fascinating cities on earth.

Even the rain doesn't keep this man from his job of cleaning a Trafalgar Square bronze lion.

The 170-foot Lord Horatio Nelson column towers over Trafalgar Square.

Lord Horatio Nelson

Lord Horatio Nelson is Britain's greatest naval hero. He was killed in the Battle of Trafalgar. His last words were, "Thank God I have done my duty." In an earlier battle, Nelson lost his right arm. The statue shows him as a one-armed man. But because the statue is 170 feet high, only the pigeons have a close enough view to notice the missing limb.

The famous pigeons of Trafalgar Square are always looking for food.

A cosmopolitan city is one in which a blend of people—rich and poor, foreign-born and native—have gathered together to live. No other city in Europe is as cosmopolitan as London. In fact, London is one of the most cosmopolitan cities in the world.

THE TRADITIONAL NEIGHBORHOODS

From the air, London's streets look like a bowl of spaghetti. They curl and swirl seemingly without purpose or aim. In the old days, many of those twisting streets were paths to village squares. The villages of old had their own markets and churches. Villagers even had their own accents. Then London gradually grew to include the old villages into one giant city. Many of the villages—which became neighborhoods—kept their old character.

The Portobello Road market is in Kensington. Shoppers there can find everything from antiques and jewelry to fruits and vegetables.

Left: A street musician with a music box and a scarlet macaw entertains shoppers.

Below: Pewter is sold at this stall.

Children in period costumes dance around a maypole in a Mayfair park.

Mayfair is a fashionable neighborhood in today's London. In the distant past, it was an open meadow. The annual May Fair was held there. London's high society people talked the king into stopping the May Fair. They said they didn't like the gambling, drinking, and wild dancing that took place there. Those rich people may just have wanted the land for themselves. As soon as the fair closed, the upper classes moved onto the old fairgrounds and built elegant homes there. Mayfair is still the wealthiest district in the city. How rich is Mayfair? One beauty shop in the neighborhood charges $200 to wash and set a woman's hair. And customers have to wait as long as three months for an appointment.

A fashionably dressed man walks his dog in Mayfair.

The East End is very different. That neighborhood stretches along the city's waterfront. For generations, the East End has been the refuge of immigrants. Its earliest immigrants were French Huguenots. They were fleeing from religious persecution in their native land. The French were followed by Jews, who also were seeking religious freedom. Then the Irish came. They were escaping from poverty in Ireland. The East End's latest immigrant populations are people from India and Pakistan. Those countries were once part of the British Empire.

These Iranian children are among the large immigrant population in London East End.

In the late 1800s, large numbers of European Jews came to London. Many settled in the East End.

Despite its history of poverty, the East End has always lured Londoners to its colorful street markets. For hundreds of years, merchants have sold bargain-basement clothing from stalls along the East End's Middlesex Street. Some people still call Middlesex Street by its old name—Petticoat Lane.

Several other streets in the neighborhood were named after goods once sold in their shops. In Brick Lane, bricks were sold. Not far away are Honey Street and Bread Street. Two others are called Stinking Lane and Bladder Alley. In the days before toilets with running water, one can imagine what went on there.

Original London, the section that was laid out by the Romans long ago, is now a neighborhood simply called the City. It is always spelled with a capital C. The City is about one square mile in size. After the heavy World War II bombing, it was rebuilt with office buildings instead of homes and apartments. It is now the financial and banking center of London. Only about 5,000 people live in the City, but during the day its population swells with half a million office workers.

The Petticoat Lane Market, held every Sunday morning, attracts a huge crowd of shoppers from every segment of society. The street is lined with stalls that sell everything from bagels to leather coats. Bakeries, of course, were once located on nearby Bread Street.

THE COLORFUL COCKNEY

Venture into the City or parts of the East End and stop for a sandwich. The waitress there might call you "Dearie," even though she has never seen you before. At one time, taxi drivers in this district addressed their male passengers as "governor" (pronounced "guv'nor"). Now, they usually use the word "mate." The people here are Cockneys, the most well known of all Londoners.

Tradition says a true Cockney has to be born within earshot of the bells of an old church in the City called St. Mary-le-Bow. Cockneys are famous for being outgoing and bold when breaking the rules of polite British society. One can imagine a Cockney dashing up to the queen and saying, "Hi, Dearie."

The most famous of all Cockney traits is their use—or misuse—of the English language. Cockneys refuse to roll their *r*'s as British gentlemen and gentlewomen are supposed to, and they speak as if the letter *h* is simply not in the alphabet. George Bernard Shaw created the most enduring of all Cockneys when he wrote his play *Pygmalion*, featuring flower-seller Eliza Doolittle. In the

Charlie Chaplin

Outrageous Cockney humor has delighted the British people for generations. The greatest of all Cockney comedians was silent-screen star Charlie Chaplin. He often took the role of an impoverished or even a homeless man. Yet he triumphed at the end of the movie. His trademarks were a battered derby hat and a bamboo cane that he twirled like a baton. In the 1920s, he was hailed as the "funniest man alive." Chaplin was a true London Cockney. He was born within earshot of the bells of St. Mary-le-Bow.

Gregor

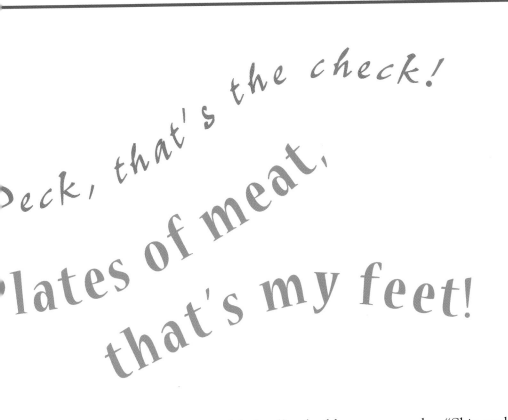

Peck, that's the check! Plates of meat, that's my feet!

...ay, Eliza meets a college ...ofessor who decides he ...n make her into a society ...oman simply by correcting ...r speech. *My Fair Lady* ...as the lively musical ...ersion of the Shaw play. A ...iumphant note in the ...usical came when Eliza ...arned the proper way to ...y, "The rain in Spain falls ...ainly in the plain." ...reviously, her words for ...ain," "Spain," and "plain" ...l rhymed with "spine."

Sadly, Cockneys are ...isappearing from London ...ulture. Their old neighbor-...ood in the City is now a maze of drab office build-ings. Children of Cockney parents have moved to other neighborhoods and have lost their special accents. Old-time Cockneys still get together to talk, however. When they social-ize or want to confuse or amuse someone within hearing, they speak a rhyming slang they created: "Plates of meat, that's my feet" is a Cockney saying. It makes no sense, but it rhymes and flows into sentences: "I been walkin' all day and my plates sure hurt." Here are more examples: "Skin and blister, that's my sister." "Gregory Peck, that's the check." A complete sentence might be: "Last night I went to a restaurant with old skin and blister, and she paid the Gregory." If you can't figure that sentence out, you aren't using your loaf. That's right, your loaf, which is made of bread and rhymes with . . .

This flower seller is doing a brisk business outside St. Mary-le-Bow.

THE IMMIGRANTS

Because it is a major seaport, foreign sailors and merchants have for centuries settled in London. Africans, for example, have lived in London for more than 500 years. Accounts say that one black man, who was a city resident in the 1500s, was famous because he was the only person in England who knew how to make steel sewing needles. But foreigners, especially nonwhites, made up only a tiny minority in the city until after World War II.

After the war, wave after wave of immigrants from all over Britain's vast empire began arriving in London. They came from India, Pakistan, and the West Indies. By the 1970s, hundreds of thousands of immigrants lived in London. Children of immigrant parents packed the schools. Then the British economy slowed, and unemployment haunted the workers. Native Londoners complained that they were forced to compete with nonwhite jobseekers who were willing to work for lower wages. After several clashes on the streets, West Indian blacks claimed that police treated them badly.

After World War II, hundreds of thousands of immigrants arrived in London. They now help to make up the city's diverse and interesting population.

The London Bobbies

London is a gentle city. It is one of the few cities in the world where policemen carry no guns. The city police are called "Bobbies." They were named after Sir Robert (Bobbie) Peel, who founded the Metropolitan Police Force in 1829.

Serious strife between the races has been rare in London, however. Everyone agrees that the immigrants have made the city the exciting melting pot it is today. They certainly added spice to the city's restaurants. Traditional British restaurant offerings such as deep-fried fish and chips are bland to the taste and heavy with grease. Since the wave of immigrants arrived, however, London restaurants have presented an amazing variety of ethnic delights. Where else in the world can one find Chinese, Indian, Vietnamese, Turkish, and Moroccan restaurants, all on the same block?

STORY

The history of a city or a country is highlighted by times of crisis and stories of heroic efforts on the part of its people. Since its beginnings, London has celebrated many such defining moments. All these are separate stories, and each could very well begin with the words, "The year was . . ."

A CITY AND A RIVER

The year was A.D. 43.

A small fleet of Roman sailing ships approached the shores of Britain. They landed at what is now Colchester, a little north of the Thames River estuary. For hundreds of years, Celtic people had lived in farming and fishing communities along the Thames. If those Roman sailors saw a Celtic village, however, they made no note of it in their reports.

The Romans quickly established a seaport settlement on the riverbanks and called it Londinium. Some historians believe it is a Celtic word meaning "strong point." Engineers built a wooden bridge across the Thames. That first London Bridge was put up at the same spot where more-famous London Bridges would appear in ages to come. To protect themselves from invaders, the settlers built a wall around Londinium. The wall, portions of which can still be seen today, enclosed about one square mile of ground.

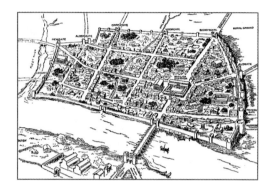

The map above shows the wall around the Roman city of Londinium.

In 55 and 54 B.C., Roman general Julius Caesar invaded Britain. It wasn't until A.D. 43, however, that the Romans founded Londinium.

20

In the early 1500s, long after the Romans had left, the city by the Thames was still largely confined to that one square mile of territory. The Thames River, which emptied into the sea, put London in a powerful position to carry on world trade. The city's merchants—who dealt in cloth, glass, pottery, wine, and fish—grew rich. Workers flocked to town, hoping to share in the prosperity. From 1530 to 1600, the number of Londoners increased threefold. England's rulers established palaces in neighboring Westminster. Soon, London expanded to include Westminster. It became one large city on the Thames.

Above: London as it looked in the early 1500s
Below (large buildings in the background, left to right): A 1647 view of Parliament House, Westminster Hall, and Westminster Abbey

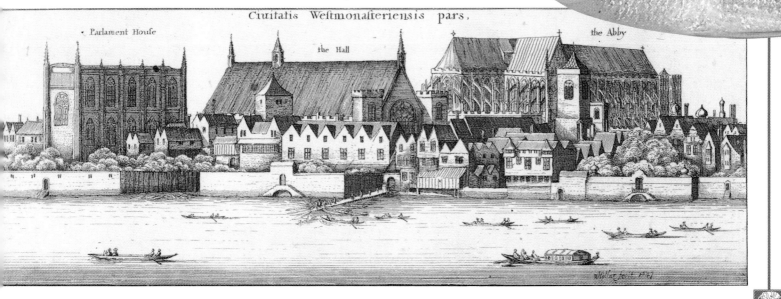

Queen Elizabeth I reigned from 1558 to 1603.

By the time of Queen Elizabeth I, who reigned from 1558 to 1603, no city in the western world could match London in size or spirit. The twisting streets of central London were a roar of sounds: horses' hooves clattering on cobblestones, dogs barking, vendors shouting out prices of the fish or cloth they sold. The great London Bridge was a neighborhood in itself. The bridge stood on a series of nineteen arches. It was crowded with houses and shops built on both sides of its walkway. In Elizabethan times, people walked across London Bridge to attend theaters in Southwark. One Southwark theater, the Globe, featured plays written by William Shakespeare.

Elizabethan London had grown so fast it was now overcrowded, filthy, and swarming with rats. One visitor from a small English town called the London of this time "a vast, unwieldy, and disorderly babble of buildings."

Old London Bridge as it looked in 1600

During Elizabethan times, the cobblestone streets of central London were crowded and noisy. This woodcut shows the Bellman of London.

William Shakespeare's plays were performed at the Globe Theater, in Southwark.

THE TWIN DISASTERS

During the plague of 1665, thousands of Londoners died (above) and thousands more fled the city in terror (below).

The year was 1665.

Hundreds of Londoners saw frightening black splotches break out just under their skin. They developed headaches, fever, and body pains. Most were dead within a matter of days. Londoners knew it was the "Black Death," the same terrifying illness that had swept Europe and England in the past. It is now called the bubonic plague. The disease was spread by fleas that lived on rats. Some 70,000 Londoners—one of every seven people in the city—died during the 1665 epidemic. Death in such huge numbers spread confusion and fear among the people. Sidewalk preachers told crowds the plague was the angry hand of God punishing Londoners for their sins. Sorcerers sold charms guaranteed to protect people from the awful sickness. Thousands of panic-stricken Londoners fled their city. Writer Daniel Defoe said, "In [the] Whitechapel [neighborhood] nothing was to be seen but wagons and carts with goods, women, children, etc. . . . a terrible and melancholy thing to see."

The Great Fire of London in 1666 burned for three days and leveled two-thirds of the huge city.

The year was 1666.

The plague had run its ~~deadly~~ course. Londoners ~~ha~~d drifted back to their ~~city~~. Then, in September, a ~~ba~~ker began making bread ~~in~~ his shop on Pudding ~~La~~ne. Somehow, the fire in ~~the~~ oven caused the kitchen ~~to~~ burst into flames. For ~~mo~~nths, the weather had ~~bee~~n very dry. Swirling ~~win~~ds rapidly spread the fire from rooftop to rooftop and from building to building in the crowded city. In a few short hours, the fire was a monster. It howled over the heart of London. Londoner John Evelyn wrote, "Oh, the miserable and calamitous spectacle! All the sky was of a fiery aspect, like the top of a burning oven. . . . God grant my eyes may never behold the like. . . . The noise and crackling and thunder of the flames, the shrieking of women and children, the hurry of people, the fall of towers, houses, and churches was like a hideous storm."

The great fire burned for three days. Miraculously, only six people were killed in the blaze. But two-thirds of the city was leveled, and 200,000 people were left homeless. The ruins were still smoking when Londoners started rebuilding. The twin disasters of plague and fire did not dampen their spirits. The greatest structure to rise in the years after the fire was St. Paul's Cathedral, designed by architect Christopher Wren. The dome of the new church dominated the city skyline for centuries to come.

THE BLITZ

The year was 1940.

London now sprawled far beyond both sides of the Thames. The city held factories, office buildings, shipping docks, and thousands of houses. The British capital in 1940 was the world's largest city, a title it had held for more than 100 years. Across the narrow English Channel, however, German dictator Adolf Hitler had just conquered France. Now he turned his eyes on Britain. Hitler dreamed of invading its shores. He first had to shatter the morale of the English people by launching massive air raids on their cities. British prime minister Winston Churchill said of Hitler and his terror tactics, "This wicked man . . . has now resolved to break our famous island race by a process of indiscriminate slaughter and destruction."

Night after night, from September 1940 to May 1941, German bombers roared over London, dropping their deadly loads. It was a time of agony that Londoners called the Blitz. Men, women, and children huddled in shelters and in subway stations while bombs shook the streets above them. The sights and sounds were horrifying: searchlights pierced the night, air-raid sirens wailed, bombs thudded, wounded and terrified people screamed. One of the worst raids took place on December 29, 1940. Incendiary bombs started 1,500 separate raging fires. Not since the Great Fire of 1666 had the city faced such terrible flames.

A famous photograph taken the next morning showed the dome of St. Paul's Cathedral, ringed with smoke, but still standing.

Cheerful Londoners give the V for victory sign after being bombed out of their home during an air raid.

British Spitfires fought back against the Germans during the Battle of Britain.

During the terrible nightly air raids of the Battle of Britain, Londoners took shelter in subway stations.

...d St. Paul's Cathedral as it ...ked the morning after one of the ...rst air raids of the Blitz

Reminders of War

The massive wreckage left from World War II air raids was cleaned up long ago, but officials at the Victoria and Albert Museum decided to leave the pockmarked outside walls unrepaired as a testament to the war's violence. As this picture shows, great chunks of the wall were knocked loose by splinters from exploding bombs.

The picture cheered Londoners. Old St. Paul's, born after the Great Fire of 1666, had lived through another major fire.

Somehow, Londoners also survived the Blitz. More than 30,000 of its citizens were killed. About 80 percent of the city's houses and other buildings were destroyed or damaged. Yet morale in the capital was high. In Germany, Adolf Hitler couldn't believe the strength of the British people. That defiance against the rain of bombs gave the nation's leaders the vital time they needed to build up their air force. Eventually, British fliers won what history came to call the Battle of Britain. That battle was Hitler's first major defeat in World War II. It marked the beginning of the end for Hitler's Nazi Germany.

arks, theaters, and restaurants are among the pleasures of life that help make London a wonderful city for leisure living. It has places to shop, places to play, and neighborhoods where residents enjoy endless activities.

STREET SONGS AND STREET GAMES

Ring-a-ring o' roses
Pocketful of posies,
Achoo, achoo, all fall down.

Nearly everyone who grows up in an English-speaking country has sung those lines. But few know that the song began during a fourteenth-century London plague. The roses refer to the red rash on the face, probably the first symptom of the plague. Carrying posies (flowers) in one's pocket was believed to protect one from the epidemic. "Achoo, achoo" refers to the final sneezing attack before death, when "all fall down."

Another famous sidewalk song, "London Bridge Is Falling Down," has several interpretations. They are all rooted in London's past. Some say the song dates to the year 1014.

*These London schoolchildre
are enjoying a field trip.*

That is when Vikings attacked the city, tore down the wooden bridge then in use, and wrote a poem about their victory. Others say the words stem from the winter of 1282. That year, portions of the stone London Bridge "fell down" after being rammed by giant chunks of ice.

British boys and girls from London and other cities sing a lively acting rhyme that honors the capital's ancient churches and buildings. The song also gives children a musical history lesson:

**Oranges and lemons
Say the bells of
St. Clements.**

Many years ago, St. Clements church had a fruit market on its grounds. A later line in the "Oranges and Lemons" song is:

**Oh, when will you
pay me?
Say the bells of
Old Bailey.**

Old Bailey was a very grim debtors' prison where people who failed to pay their bills were locked up. The song ends on a grisly note, reminding us that beheading was once a common form of execution in England:

**Here comes the
candle to light you
to bed,
Here comes the
chopper to chop off
your head.
Chop, Chop, Chop,
Chop . . .**

During the rhyme, two children make an arch with their arms. The rest of the children walk under the arch until the end. The last child is caught and "executed" when the arms come down around him or her. That child and a partner then form an arch and the game continues.

The second London Bridge was built of stone. It looked like this in 1209.

A game called "conkers" is an autumn craze among London children. The equipment is simple: some horse chestnuts—which grow on trees in the parks—and a few lengths of string. Each player punches a hole in a horse chestnut—the conker—and attaches a length of string to it. One player is chosen to be "up," as in "batter up." Others must let their horse chestnuts dangle on strings while, one by one, the "up" player swings at them with his conker. The object is to shatter the opposing horse chestnut. The player with the last conker remaining in one piece wins the game. The winner must be paid with a freshly picked batch of horse chestnuts.

These boys are having a conkers contest. It is a popular game among London children in the autumn, when chestnuts (conkers) are plentiful.

Rounders is a team game played by boys and girls in London parks and on school grounds. The action begins with a bowler (pitcher) throwing a ball toward a player who tries to hit it with a stick (rounder's bat). After hitting the ball, the player runs to one of four corner bases. If this game sounds familiar to Americans, it should. Many years ago, the English brought rounders to the New World, and it evolved into American baseball. Rugby, another English game brought to America, evolved into American football.

*ese children are playing
cket in Kensington Park.
icket, played with balls
d bats, is one of the most
pular games in England.*

Rugby, being played here in Regent's Park, was the origin of the American game of football.

THE THEATER

The Drury Lane, the Garrick, the London Palladium, the Savoy, Wyndham's—all these are famous London theaters. London is the greatest theater center in the English-speaking world. Going to the theater is a part of the city's culture. Boys and girls start attending performances before they reach age ten. Most will remain theater fans for life. Londoners expect—and usually get— the best in dramatic and musical entertainment.

This London theater is showing production of Phantom of the Opera.

Shaftesbury Avenue, shown here, is part of the London Theater District.

Agatha Christie's play The Mousetrap *is the longest-running mystery ever performed in the Theater District. This group was celebrating the thirty-eighth year of the run. In 1996, a forty-fourth anniversary will be celebrated.*

Lavish musicals featuring casts of fifty or more performers are favorite events in the capital. Extravaganzas such as *Miss Saigon* and *Les Misérables* were hits in the 1990s. Comic operettas written by the beloved team of Gilbert and Sullivan are shown at many London theaters. In the late 1800s, Gilbert and Sullivan won the hearts of English theatergoers by gently poking fun at British society. In one of their songs, a naval officer claims that he rose to high rank by mindlessly following orders and never thinking for himself: "I thought so little they rewarded me / By making me the ruler of the Queen's navee."

The most popular theaters are concentrated along Charing Cross Road, St. Martin's Lane, and Shaftesbury Avenue. This section of town is called the Theater District. The neighborhood offers theater lovers delightful choices—comedies, serious dramas, musicals, and mysteries. The most enduring mystery ever performed in the Theater District is an Agatha Christie play called *The Mousetrap*. In 1995, it began its forty-third straight year of performances. And, night after night, *The Mousetrap* still plays to packed houses. The plays of William Shakespeare are a national institution in Great Britain. Some of the world's best Shakespearean actors and actresses perform with London's Royal Shakespeare Company.

THE PARKS

As far back as 1800, aristocrat William Pitt declared, "Parks are the lungs of London." Londoners cherish their parks as grand places to unwind from city madness. The parks are kept clean, the grass is cut regularly, and flower beds are carefully tended. The capital has more than eighty major parks. The best loved are the large inner-city parks—Kensington Gardens, Hyde Park, Green Park, St. James's, and Regent's Park. These are Royal Parks. That means they were once private hunting and picnic grounds owned by the Royal Family. Over the centuries, various kings and queens opened them to public use. Thus, the Royal Parks lie in the oldest neighborhoods and serve as quiet, green islands in the midst of the busy city.

These families are enjoying a Sunday afternoon boat ride on Hyde Park's Serpentine Lake.

Sunday afternoon is a favorite time for Londoners to enjoy a picnic in the park.

In the Royal Parks and in other nature reserves, men and women walk, jog, or ride bicycles or horses. Children zip over the walkways on skateboards and roller blades. Kite flying is a favorite springtime activity. Each park has features that have been enjoyed by London families for so long they are looked upon as birthrights for every city dweller. Hyde Park and Kensington Gardens are graced by the finger-shaped Serpentine Lake. Regent's Park is home to an open-air theater and to the London Zoo.

St. James's has a beautiful tree-lined lake.

This lucky boy is getting a roller-skate ride from his sister.

Every Sunday afternoon, an organized shouting match takes place at Speakers' Corner in Hyde Park. Want to be saved? Or save the whales? Or ban the bomb? Just come to Speakers' Corner on a Sunday afternoon. Bring a box—an empty milk crate will do. Turn the box over, stand on it, and shout for your cause. Better shout loud. Eight or ten other speakers will be blaring out their messages at the same time. Many of those who speak are religious preachers. The best of them draw large crowds. Heckling is permitted and even encouraged at Speakers' Corner. Hecklers try to belittle or insult the speakers. Often the crowds pay more attention to the heckler than they do to the man or woman preaching on the box. A speaker might be raving about the joys of a vegetarian diet and denouncing red meat as the world's greatest evil. A heckler will shout, "Hey, meet me at McDonald's. I'll buy you a burger." The crowd laughs. The heckler has scored a point.

This Christian evangelist is preaching at Hyde Park's Speakers' Corner.

Every Sunday afternoon, crowds gather to listen to the soapbox orators at Speakers' Corner in Hyde Park.

Aside from Sundays in that corner of Hyde Park, the parks are peaceful places. Crime on their grounds is almost nonexistent. The Royal Parks are large enough for a stroller to escape from the noise and fumes of traffic. In 1852—when the city was sleepy compared to today—poet Matthew Arnold used to go to London parks to compose his verses. While sitting in Kensington Gardens, amid the grass and trees and flowers, Arnold wrote:

> *Calm soul of all things! Make it mine*
> *To feel, amid the city's jar,*
> *That there abides a peace of thine*
> *Man did not make, and cannot mar.*

These people are relaxing and enjoying the flowers and fresh air at Greenwich Park.

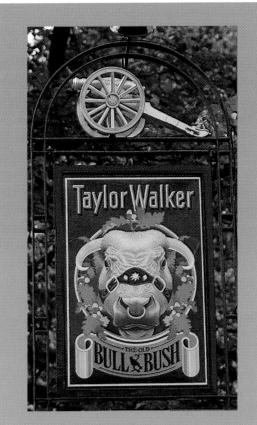

The Pub

Many Londoners spend some of their leisure hours at the "pub," short for public house. Pubs are places to enjoy a beer and chat with one's neighbors. Most pubs serve food, often called "pub grub." Pub food may include fish and chips, steak and kidney pie, bangers and mash (sausages and mashed potatoes), and shepherd's pie. In many pubs, cheese, bread, and salads are also on the menu.

CITY

W hen a man is tired of London, he is tired of life; for there is in London all that life can afford.

Samuel Johnson, writing in 1777

THE CITY

At the edge of the City rises the Tower of London, a place alive with history and legend. In 1066, French nobleman William the Conqueror invaded England and took control of the country. William built a watchtower to keep an eye on his newly won prize, the city of London. That first structure evolved into the Tower of London, a group of stone buildings enclosed by a wall.

Over the centuries, the Tower has been used as a fortress, a palace, and a prison. In its role as a prison, it contained a torture chamber with walls sixteen inches thick. The oversized walls muffled the screams of torture victims. The Tower was also the site of executions by beheading, strangulation, and many more hideous methods. King Henry VIII, who reigned in the 1500s, had two of his wives executed at the Tower. The wives had displeased the king, and at the time, divorce was not permitted.

Beefeaters like the man pictured at lower left guard the Tower of London.

The display of armor shown below is part of the Tower's huge collection of arms and armor.

Today, thousands of people come to the Tower to see the Crown Jewels. It is a breathtaking collection of diamonds, rubies, and glittering gold. Among the collection is the Imperial State Crown. It was made in 1838 and contains some 2,800 diamonds. Some who see the crown might envy royalty and the riches they possess. Throughout history, however, Britain's kings and queens have complained that crowns feel heavy on their heads and give them a headache after only a few minutes.

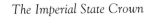

The Imperial State Crown

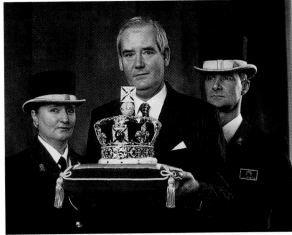

The Tower of London

Anyone walking up the Thames River from the Tower will encounter an ordinary (some say ugly-looking) bridge. It is London Bridge, or at least the present version of that structure. The first bridge at this spot was built by the Romans nearly 2,000 years ago. The most enduring London Bridge was constructed here in 1176. It lasted for 655 years. Another London Bridge, built in 1831, gave way to the present bridge, which was put up in the early 1970s.

The fate of the old London Bridge—the 1831 structure —brings smiles to many Londoners. The 1831 bridge was bought by an American oil company. It was shipped stone by stone across the ocean, to be reassembled in Arizona. The oil company wanted to create a tourist magnet on the Arizona sands. But wait! Did the American oil millionaires buy the wrong bridge? Tower Bridge stands farther downstream. It is a structure so famous and so frequently photographed that at first glance, visitors sometimes point to it and say, "Look, there's London Bridge." There were rumors that the oil company executives made that same tourist blunder. They then had to complete the purchase because they were too embarrassed to admit having made such a colossal mistake.

A fireworks display at Tower Bridge

A businessman in a bowler hat passes the London Stock Exchange.

THE STOCK EXCHANGE

Architect Christopher Wren created both St. Paul's Cathedral (left) and the Monument to the Great Fire of 1666 (below).

The City is a business and banking center. Its skyline is dominated by modern office buildings. A glorious exception to this forest of glass and steel is St. Paul's Cathedral. It is the greatest work of architect Christopher Wren. St. Paul's massive dome, its portico, and its broad steps have awed Londoners since the building was completed in 1710. Another Christopher Wren creation—the Monument—stands nearby at the spot where the Great Fire of 1666 began. A 202-foot column with a golden crown of sculpted flames, the Monument was built to commemorate the fire. More than any other architect, Christopher Wren left his signature on London. He is buried at St. Paul's. On his tomb are words in Latin that declare his impact on the great city: "Reader, if you seek his monument, look around you."

SOUTH OF THE RIVER

South London is the district that lies south of the Thames. It is often overlooked by tourists. But in the 1600s and 1700s, the community south of London Bridge was the city's pleasure quarters. It was a place of theaters, taverns, and gambling dens. Religious groups closed the theaters, calling them "chapels of Satan." In the 1800s, South London became an industrial slum. Then, in the 1980s and 1990s, several exciting projects were launched, and now the tourists are returning.

One of South London's most exciting new undertakings is the construction of the Globe Theater. Built near the site of the old Globe, the theater is a replica of the one that stood in 1599. That was the theater that featured the works of William Shakespeare. Like the original Globe, the new one is built of oak beams held together with wooden pegs. The open-roofed central area provides standing room for theatergoers. It is surrounded by thatched-roof galleries with seats. The roofed areas in the original theater were used by those patrons who could afford seats.

Above: Visitors tour the Globe Theater in South London.

Left: An aerial view of London, the Thames River, and Tower Bridge in a raised position

Near London Bridge is the London Dungeon Museum. The museum depicts the horrors of long-ago prison life. Its displays include torture instruments such as the rack. Despite its terrible theme, the London Dungeon Museum always has long lines of people

It's fun to tour London in one of the famous red double-decker buses.

The Tube

London's public transportation is clean, safe, and efficient. The red double-decker bus is a city trademark. The fastest way to get from place to place is on the Underground. This below-ground train system is popularly called the Tube. The London Underground network is the world's largest.

...iting to get in and study ...exhibits. Children are the ...ost enthusiastic visitors.

The Imperial War ...useum has displays of ...eapons used in wars— ...nks, heavy guns, and a ...erman V-2 rocket. The ...splays do not glorify war. ...one corner, visitors walk through a World War I trench where they see models of troops living in mud. Then guests are led into a mock-up of a World War II London air-raid shelter. Sitting in the dark shelter, visitors hear the thunder of bombs and feel the ground tremble. Finally, the raid is over. An air-raid warden leads the people out into bombed-out streets whose topsy-turvy buildings still smolder from a dozen fires. The simulated air attack is a chilling reminder of war's horrors.

THE WEST END

The West End, west of the City, is tourists' London. Here are the grand monuments, the museums, the elegant shops, theaters, and restaurants. The West End is part of the city of Westminster. Historic Westminster Abbey, where Britain's kings and queens have been crowned for the past 900 years, is a legacy from the old city. Next to it are the Houses of Parliament, also called the Palace of Westminster. They stand majestically along the Thames. One of London's great landmarks is the giant ornate clock tower that rises out of the Parliament building. It houses the famous brass bell called Big Ben.

Just off Whitehall is Downing Street. Its famous address—No. 10 Downing Street—is home of the British prime minister.

A streetside souvenir stand

The Clock Tower houses the famous bell called Big Ben.

The House of Lords meets in this ornate chamber in the Houses of Parliament.

The Houses of Parliament

One of the beautiful Gothic-style doors to Westminster Abbey

Buckingham Palace is the official home of the British monarch. It is easy to tell if the queen is in residence on a given day. When Her Majesty is at home, the Royal Ensign flies from the palace roof. Buckingham Palace is a number-one destination for tourists. They gather in front of its walls at 11 A.M. to watch the Changing of the Guard. The guard ceremony is full of the pomp and pageantry that the British are so famous for. During the ceremony, a military band plays while soldiers march stiffly to the palace gates. In the summer, the soldiers wear red jackets and bearskin hats. The winter time uniform is plain khaki. The historic Changing of the Guard takes place every day during the summer, and every other day during the winter months.

Buckingham Palace is the official home of the British monarch.

The famous Buckingham Palace Guards in their red summer uniforms and bearskin hats

Harrods, London's most famous department store, sells its own brand of tea.

The West End is a marvelous place to shop, or at least to window-shop. Prices at the prestigious stores are very high. One store, Harrods, is so elegant that members of the Royal Family are regular customers there. Don't expect to bump into the queen in the ladies' hat department, though. When the queen visits, the management opens the store an hour early to accommodate her.

London's finest museums are clustered in the West End. These include the Royal Academy of the Arts, the Natural

Right: Queen Elizabeth and Prince Philip are portrayed in wax at Madame Tussaud's Waxworks, a museum in the West End.

Below: An artist works on a wax image of Prime Minister Winston Churchill.

tory Museum, the ence Museum, and the toria and Albert seum (which displays orative art). Near gent's Park is Madame saud's Waxworks, a seum that has enjoyed raordinary popularity for ost 200 years. Madame Tussaud's displays remarkably lifelike wax figures of people such as boxer Muhammad Ali or movie character Indiana Jones. The museum is famous mainly for its depictions of sinister criminals the likes of Jack the Ripper, the serial killer who prowled the streets of London in 1888.

The British Museum in the heart of the West End is truly one of the world's great museums.

It was founded in 1753 and experienced its greatest growth during the mid-1800s. That is when the British Empire reached its zenith. The museum displays objects of antiquity collected from all the lands touched upon by England's empire-building crusade. In a special gallery are magnificent marble statues that date to 450 B.C. They once graced the Parthenon in Athens, Greece.

Also shown is the Rosetta Stone, which bears a religious message in three ancient languages. The stone provided a vital key for scholars struggling to understand the long-forgotten language of the Egyptians. The museum grounds cover fourteen

Left: A few of London's most elegant shops deliver merchandise to customers in horse-drawn carriages.

Above: The Egyptology display at the British Museum

res and the building holds ore than 4 million items. ly a fraction of its hibits can be seen in a gle visit.

Also in the West End is rafalgar Square, a place here many people begin or d a visit to London. The uare recalls the time of empire, when London was the capital of the world. London no longer commands an empire. But many travelers come to Trafalgar Square, stand under the column of Lord Nelson, and proclaim that London remains the world's most exciting city.

Above: Red double-decker buses line Oxford Street on a busy day.

Right: The Lord Nelson column in Trafalgar Square

FAMOUS LANDMARKS

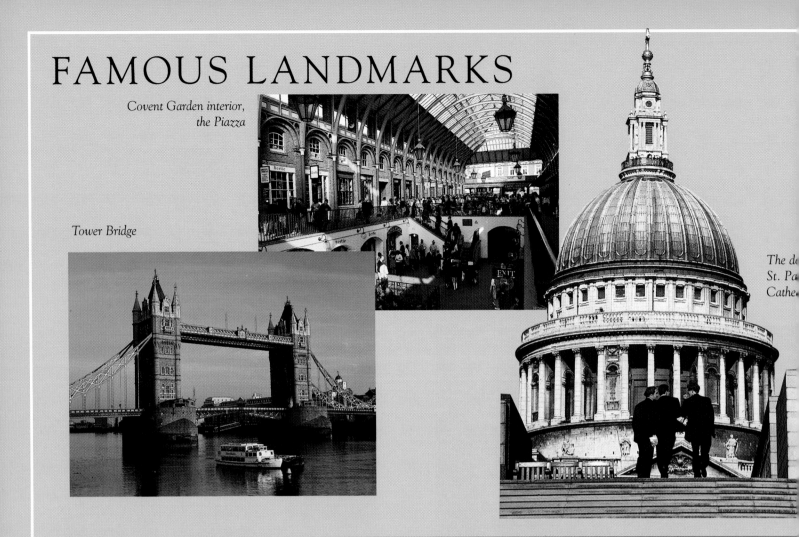

Covent Garden interior, the Piazza

Tower Bridge

The de
St. Pa
Cathe

Tower of London
Located on the eastern edge of the City, the Tower of London was begun by William the Conqueror shortly after he invaded England in 1066. It is now a museum that contains the Crown Jewels. On view near the Tower is a portion of a Roman wall built nearly 2,000 years ago.

Tower Bridge
A symbol of London since it was completed in 1894, the middle span of the bridge is raised and lowered like an elevator to permit the passage of ships.

Southwark Cathedral
A marvelous church that dates back to A.D. 1220, it served the town (now the borough) of Southwark. William Shakespeare's younger brother Edmund is buried there, and John Harvard, the founder of Harvard University in the United States, was baptized in the church in 1608.

The Monument
Designed by Christopher Wren, the Monument, which commemorates the Great Fire of 1666, is a white column 202 feet high. It stands exactly 202 feet from the spot where the fire broke out. If tipped over in the proper direction, its crown would touch the bakery shop that was once on Pudding Lane and where the disastrous blaze began.

St. Paul's Cathedral
The greatest work of Christopher Wren (who designed 55 other London churches), it survived the heavy bombing of World War II and continues to inspire Londoners.

Imperial War Museum
In the Lambeth neighborhood, the museum displays weapons exhibits of recent wars.

Covent Garden
England's Royal Opera House, building is known for its lush orations outside and its superb acoustics inside.

British Museum
Truly one of the great museums all the world, its exhibits inclu pottery from Sumeria, Egyptian mummies, classical Greek statu Roman statues and coins, the Rosetta Stone, an original copy the Magna Carta, and much m

Piccadilly Circus

Westminster Abbey

The Clock Tower and Big Ben at the Houses of Parliament

atural History Museum
ened in 1881, this beautiful
seum and research center in
uth Kensington was designed by
red Waterhouse. Museum
hibits include an Ecology
llery complete with a rain forest.

ndon Zoo
uated in Regent's Park, the zoo
a popular place for family
tings. Visitors can reach the
by public barge from Little
nice or Camden Lock.

Piccadilly Circus
Not a circus with trapeze artists
and the like, Piccadilly is, instead,
an intersection of four streets in
the heart of the West End. It is
often referred to as the Times
Square of London. In the center
of this urban plaza rises the statue
of Eros.

Royal Academy of Arts
Near Piccadilly Circus, the
Academy has a wonderful
permanent collection and hosts
many visiting art exhibitions.
Each summer for 200 years, the
Academy has held an exhibition
of new works by artists both
known and unknown.

Science Museum
Also in South Kensington,
opposite the Victoria and Albert
Museum, this museum displays
scientific discoveries and
inventions from the late 1800s to
the present. Many of the exhibits
are interactive.

St. James's Church
Also near Piccadilly Circus, St.
James's is another glorious exam-
ple of Christopher Wren's work.

Houses of Parliament
Standing gracefully along the
Thames, the Parliament grounds
also incorporate two other landmarks—Westminster Abbey and
the Clock Tower that houses Big
Ben.

Buckingham Palace
The official royal residence since
1837, the palace is noted for its
Changing of the Guard ceremony.

The Tate Gallery
A splendid art museum that
displays paintings from 1500 to
modern times.

FAST FACTS

POPULATION   1994
Greater London: 6,767,500
In terms of population, London is now the 17th-largest city in the world. Throughout the 1800s and the opening decades of the 1900s, it was the world's largest city.

AREA Greater London: 610 sq. miles

GOVERNMENT London is a collection of villages that over the years evolved into neighborhoods, or boroughs. The British capital has 32 separate boroughs, each with its own elected mayor and council members. The City (ancient London) is governed by a Lord Mayor and 24 aldermen.

CLIMATE Rain and mist prevail much of the year. Snow is rare in London. The average January temperature is 39 degrees Fahrenheit. The average July temperature is 63 degrees Fahrenheit.

INDUSTRIES London has long been Britain's leading city for manufacturing, trade, and finance. More than half a million people (17 percent of the nation's industrial workforce) work in its factories. Electrical machinery and instruments are leading products, followed by printing, clothing, processed food products, and furniture. Through all its history, London has been a major seaport. Until World War II, most of its wharves and docks were strung along the Thames River just east of London Bridge. Now the busiest docks are in the outer suburb of Tilbury, which has facilities to load and unload modern container ships. Banking and insurance firms are concentrated in the City. Also in the City is the London Stock Exchange, one of the world's biggest. Some 700,000 Londoners work in finance, insurance, or banking.

CHRONOLOGY

A.D. 43
The Romans build a settlement, Londinium, on the banks of the Thames and the English (Anglo-Saxons) begin to arrive

410
Roman soldiers and sailors leave Londinium

797
The Danes invade the village of London

1066
William the Conqueror invades and occupies England; William begins construction of the Tower of London

1348–49
The bubonic plague—the Black Death—strikes London

1665
Once more, the plague sweeps the city, killing one in seven inhabitants

1666
The Great Fire of London destroys two-thirds of the city

1710
St. Paul's Cathedral, the most famous church designed by architect Christopher Wren, is completed

An evening mist in Parliament Square

50
ndon expands toward the ighboring city of Westminster

305
rd Horatio Nelson defeats the nch and Spanish fleets near pe Trafalgar on the coast of ain

1831
Construction begins on London Bridge, replacing an older bridge that had served for more than 600 years

1837
Buckingham Palace becomes the official residence of the Royal Family

1915
World War I German blimps, called zeppelins, attack London

1940
The Blitz begins and Londoners endure nightly air raids that kill 30,000 of its residents and damage 80 percent of its buildings

1953
Elizabeth II is crowned in Westminster Abbey

1995
Londoners celebrate the 50th anniversary of V.E. Day, the defeat of Nazi Germany, and V.J. Day, the surrender of Japan

LONDON

London Zoo
Regent's Park
Madame Tussaud's Waxworks
St. Mary-le-Bow
British Museum
THE CITY
St. Paul's Cathedral
Middlesex Street
Brick Lane
WEST END
London Palladium
COVENT GARDEN
Charing Cross Rd
St. Clements Church
EAST END
MAYFAIR
Shaftesbury Av.
St. Martin's Lane
Drury Lane Theater
Speaker's Corner
Royal Academy of the Arts
Piccadilly Circus
Savoy Theater
Thames River
The Monument
Hyde Park
St. James's Church
Trafalgar Square
National Film Theater
Globe Theater
London Bridge
Tower Bridge
Southwark Cathedral
Serpentine Lake
Downing Street (Number Ten)
London Dungeon Museum
Kensington Gardens
Green Park
St. James's Park
SOUTH LONDON
Science Museum
Harrods
Buckingham Palace
Westminster Abbey
Big Ben
Houses of Parliament (Palace of Westminster)
Victoria and Albert Museum
Natural History Museum
Imperial War Museum
WESTMINSTER
Tate Gallery

L   M   N   O

LONDON AND SURROUNDINGS

The gold rectangle in the center of this map is the area shown in the page 60 map.

GLOSSARY

aspiring: To have a strong ambition or to want something earnestly

Celtic: Of an ancient people, the Celts, who inhabited the British Isles and much of Western Europe

conflagration: A great fire

depiction: A drawing or representation of an image

epidemic: The rapid spread of a disease

fascinating: Very interesting; charming; enchanting

heckle: To ridicule or make fun of a speaker

immigrant: A person who has moved from his or her homeland to settle in a foreign country

melancholy: Sadness, a low-spirited mood

pewter: A metal made from tin and copper

plentiful: More than enough

portico: A grand porch supported by columns

protest: To object strongly

refuge: A hiding place or getaway spot

reign: A period of rule for a king or queen

vital: Necessary

zenith: A high point for a society or a nation

Picture Identifications

Cover: The Imperial State Crown; a London phone booth; the Tower of London; a Beefeater (Yeoman of the Guard)
Page 1: Students on a class trip
Pages 4-5: Trafalgar Square
Pages 8-9: Spectators at the procession that followed the wedding of Prince Andrew and Sarah Ferguson
Pages 18-19: Prime Minister Winston Churchill inspecting damage done by an air raid during the Blitz
Pages 28-29: Londoners enjoying St. James's Park in the spring
Pages 40-41: A band playing at the Changing of the Guard ceremony at Buckingham Palace
Page 41: A girl feeding the pigeons in Trafalgar Square

Photo Credits

ABOUT THE AUTHOR

R. Conrad Stein was born and grew up in Chicago. After serving in the Marine Corps, he attended the University of Illinois where he received a degree in history. He later gained an advanced degree from the University of Guanajuato in Mexico. Mr. Stein is a full-time writer who has published more than 80 books for young readers. He lives in Chicago with his wife and their daughter, Janna.

London is the author's favorite city in all the world. He has traveled there several times and finds the city more exciting with each visit. Mr. Stein wishes to thank his friend Hank Eynatten, a London resident, for many enjoyable tours of the British capital.

BROTHERS

Michael Mazo   illustrated by   Michael Soloviov

Tundra Books

Published in Canada by Tundra Books,
75 Sherbourne Street, Toronto, Ontario M5A 2P9

Published in the United States by Tundra Books of Northern New York,
P.O. Box 1030, Plattsburgh, New York 12901

Library of Congress Control Number: 2008909728

Library and Archives Canada Cataloguing in Publication

Mazo, Michael
    Brothers / Michael Mazo ; Michael Soloviov, illustrator.

ISBN 978-0-88776-922-1

    I. Soloviov, Michael II. Title.

PZ7.M478Br 2009 813.'6 C2008-906637-5

We acknowledge the financial support of the Government of Canada through the Book Publishing Industry Development Program (BPIDP) and that of the Government of Ontario through the Ontario Media Development Corporation's Ontario Book Initiative. We further acknowledge the support of the Canada Council for the Arts and the Ontario Arts Council for our publishing program.

 ONTARIO ARTS COUNCIL
CONSEIL DES ARTS DE L'ONTARIO

Design: Andrew Roberts

Printed and bound in China

1 2 3 4 5 6   14 13 12 11 10 09

The Leaving

Mother has left. The dog sitter has come.

We are to be "Good Little Lambies."

6

Alpha

I am Julius the Elder, Top Dog the First. I must
work tirelessly to maintain my status, now that
William the Upstart is here. William is my little
brother. He has much to learn.
So has the sitter.

Grasshopper

William is a bouncy boy. In order to de-bounce him, I insist that he meditate daily. "Grasshopper," I tell him, "inhale inner peace. Exhale excess tension. Think: What is the sound of one paw scratching? If a wolf howls alone in the forest, does he make any noise?" Of course, there are no answers to life's great mysteries, but do not tell Grasshopper. You will disturb his profound thoughts.

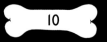

Silly Fool

My favorite part of the day is when William the Upstart tries to run through the glass doors to the patio. It makes me feel like a wise old dog to sit in my chair and laugh just loud enough for him to hear. Silly pup. When will he ever learn to test with the tip of his nose rather than the whole of his body?

Magic

Do you remember when you believed in magic?
William still does. He thinks the toilet is the
Fountain of Youth and not a drinking bowl at all.
He insists that when he's tall enough, he will
drink from it and remain eternally young.
Me, I am tall enough, and I do drink from it.
If it were magic, would I look like this?
Tell me the truth: Do you think my tail is too fat?

The Empire
vs.
The Republic

These are challenging times. William has a rebellious streak and does not accept that I am the supreme power. I have always been (and will remain) the first to receive treats, tennis balls, and behind-the-ear scratches. As a result, our den has become a place of constant tension. Negotiations often stall. William refuses to acknowledge me as sovereign; I refuse to believe in his right to exist. Most often we snarl viciously, but sometimes we form a temporary truce in order to regroup – and chew the sofa.

The Wall

When William and I can't get along, the sitter
decides we should play separately. She divides
the yard in two equal parts and leaves a dormant
Water-snake Beast in plain view, should one of us
happen to be considering a dash for freedom. By
interfering in our brotherly spat, she has merely
united us in a common cause. It is us against her.
This wall will fall.

Victory

The sitter's tour of duty is nearing an end. Today, because we have been "good dogs," she takes us to the park. There are tennis courts in the park. And in those tennis courts are tennis balls—a limitless supply of joy! She does not seem to understand that tennis balls are more important than life itself! What happens is not our fault. Our raid is unexpected and utterly unstoppable. It is not greed that inspires us to stuff forty tennis balls into our mouths—it is ambition. Our destiny is to become Wimbledon Champions. We are certain of it. Mother will be so proud.

The Homecoming

Mother has returned! The sitter is gone.

There are surprises for "Good Little Lambies."

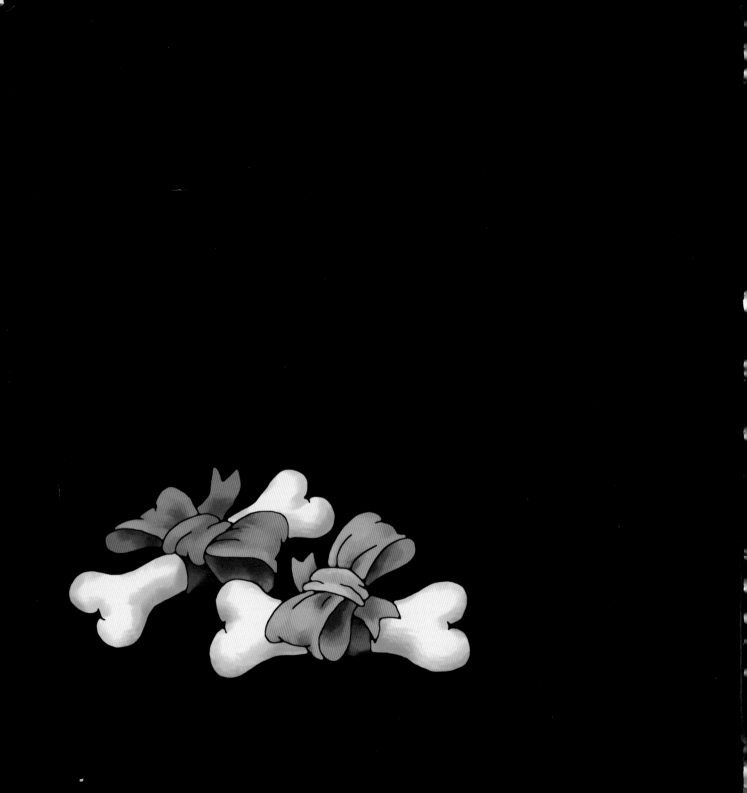